life

+ APPLICATION

MW00593162

66 quote

Prayer + Praise

ken

TAKEAWAYS

TURE: _____ date. [   ]

or: _____ audience _____

Notes

This Journal Belongs to:

Written on My Heart Journal
© DaySpring Cards, Inc. All rights reserved.
Artwork © Shanna Noel. Used by permission.
First Edition, September 2018

Published by:

P.O. Box 1010
Siloam Springs, AR 72761
dayspring.com

Designed by: Müllerhaus

Printed in China
Prime: 91511
ISBN: 9781684086702

written on my heart.

BIBLE STUDY NOTES

LIVE YOUR FAITH

Hiya!

Shanna Noel here! Welcome to your new "Written On My Heart" Bible Study Companion journal. Please note: the following pages belong to you and you alone. This is your space to be free, open and completely honest about how God is working in your life. So, don't hold back! Grab your pen, ask God to show up, open your heart and Bible, let the truth soak in, and give Him the reigns to fill you with all the joy, hope and love you could ever imagine.

SCRIPTURE: _____ date [____]

author: _____ audience _____

Notes

✝

✝

✝   ✝

[written on my ♡:]

life
APPLICATION

reminds ME OF:

_____
_____
_____
_____
_____
_____
_____
_____

" quotes "

Prayer + Praise

key
TAKEAWAYS

· · · · · · · · amen. ♥

SCRIPTURE: _____ date [____]

author: _____ audience _____

Notes

written on my ♡: [✏ _____]

life APPLICATION

reminds ME OF:

" *quotes* "

Prayer + Praise

key TAKEAWAYS

. . . . amen. ♥

SCRIPTURE: _____ date [____]

author: _____ audience _____

Notes

written on my ♥:

life

_+_ APPLICATION

reminds ME OF:

" quotes "

Prayer + Praise

key + TAKEAWAYS

.... amen. ♥

SCRIPTURE: _____ date [ ]

author: _____ audience _____

Notes

written on my ♡:

+ life

APPLICATION

reminds
ME OF:

_____
_____
_____
_____
_____
_____
_____
_____
_____

" quotes "

Prayer + Praise

key
TAKEAWAYS

· · · · · · · · amen. ♥

author: _____ audience _____

Notes

written on my ♡:

+ life +
APPLICATION

reminds ME OF:

66 quotes 99

Prayer + Praise

key
TAKEAWAYS

. . . . amen. ♥

SCRIPTURE: _____ date [____]

author: _____ audience _____

Notes

written on my ♡:

life

+ APPLICATION

reminds ME OF:

" *quotes* "

Prayer + Praise

key TAKEAWAYS

········· amen. ♥

SCRIPTURE: _____ **date** [ ]

author: _____ audience _____

Notes

✝

✝   ✝

[written on my ♥:]
[✏]

life
APPLICATION

reminds ME OF:

" quotes "

Prayer + Praise

key
TAKEAWAYS

.... amen. ♥

SCRIPTURE: _____ date [_____]

author: _____ _____ audience _____

Notes

written on my ♡:

+ life

+ APPLICATION

reminds

ME OF:

" quotes "

_____
_____
_____
_____
_____
_____
_____
_____

Prayer + Praise

Key +

TAKEAWAYS

. . . . amen. ♥

SCRIPTURE: _____ **date** [ ]

author: _____ audience _____

Notes

written on my ♥:

life APPLICATION

reminds ME OF:

" quotes "

Prayer + Praise

key TAKEAWAYS

. . . . amen. ♥

SCRIPTURE: _____ date [____]

author: _____ audience _____

Notes

✝

[written on my ♥:]

life
+ **APPLICATION**

+

reminds ME OF:

" **quotes** "

Prayer + Praise

. . . . *amen.* ♥

Key
+ **TAKEAWAYS**

SCRIPTURE: _____ date [_____]

author: _____ audience _____

Notes

[written on my ♥:]

life
+ APPLICATION

+ reminds
ME OF:

66 quotes 99

Prayer + Praise

key
TAKEAWAYS

.... amen. ♥

SCRIPTURE: _____ date [____]

author: _____ audience _____

Notes

[written on my ♡:]

life
APPLICATION

reminds
ME OF:

66 quotes 99

Prayer + Praise

key
TAKEAWAYS

. . . . amen. ♥

author: _____ audience _____

Notes

+

+

+

written on my ♡:

life
APPLICATION

reminds ME OF:

" quotes "

Prayer + Praise

key TAKEAWAYS

. . . . amen. ♥

SCRIPTURE: _____ date [____]

author: _____ audience _____

Notes

written on my ♡:

life

+ reminds ME OF:

+ APPLICATION

66 quotes 99

Prayer + Praise

key
+ TAKEAWAYS

········ amen. ♥

author: _____ audience _____

Notes

written on my ♡:

life + APPLICATION

reminds ME OF:

" quotes "

_____
_____
_____
_____
_____
_____
_____
_____

Prayer + Praise

key + TAKEAWAYS

. . . . amen. ♥

SCRIPTURE: _____ date [_____]

author: _____ audience _____

Notes

written on my ♥:

life + application

reminds me of:

quotes

_____
_____
_____
_____
_____
_____
_____
_____
_____

Prayer + Praise

key

TAKEAWAYS

. . . . amen. ♥

author: _____ audience _____

Notes

written on my ♡: _____

life

+ APPLICATION

reminds ME OF:

" quotes "

key TAKEAWAYS

Prayer + Praise

. . . . amen. ♥

SCRIPTURE: _____ date [____]

author: _____ audience _____

Notes

written on my ♡: [✏ _____]

life

+ APPLICATION

reminds ME OF:

" quotes "

Prayer + Praise

key
+ TAKEAWAYS

. . . . amen. ♥

SCRIPTURE: _____ date [____]

author: _____ audience _____

Notes

✝

✝   ✝

written on my ♡:

life
APPLICATION

reminds ME OF:

" quotes "

Prayer + Praise

key TAKEAWAYS

.... amen. ♥

SCRIPTURE: _____ date [_____]

author: _____ audience _____

Notes

written on my ♡:

life + APPLICATION

reminds ME OF:

_____
_____
_____
_____
_____
_____
_____
_____

" quotes "

Prayer + Praise

key TAKEAWAYS +

. . . . amen. ♥

SCRIPTURE: _____ **date** [____]

author: _____ audience _____

Notes

[written on my ♡:]

life + APPLICATION

reminds ME OF:

" quotes "

_____
_____
_____
_____
_____
_____
_____
_____

Prayer + Praise

key TAKEAWAYS +

. . . . amen. ♥

SCRIPTURE: _____ date [ ]

author: _____ audience _____

Notes

[written on my ♥:]

+ life +
APPLICATION

reminds
ME OF:

_____
_____
_____
_____
_____
_____
_____
_____
_____

66 quotes 99

Prayer + Praise

key +
TAKEAWAYS

. . . . amen. ♥

SCRIPTURE: _____ date [____]

author: _____ audience _____

Notes

written on my ♥:

life

+ APPLICATION

reminds ME OF:

" quotes "

Prayer + Praise

key + TAKEAWAYS

. . . . amen. ♥

SCRIPTURE: _____ **date** [_____]

author: _____ audience _____

Notes

written on my ♡:

+life+
APPLICATION

reminds ME OF:

_____
_____
_____
_____
_____
_____
_____
_____
_____
_____
_____

66 quotes 99

Prayer + Praise

key+ TAKEAWAYS

.... amen. ♥

SCRIPTURE: _____ date [____]

author: _____ audience _____

Notes

✝

✝   ✝

written on my ♡:

life

APPLICATION

reminds ME OF:

66 quotes 99

_____
_____
_____
_____
_____
_____
_____
_____

Prayer + Praise

key TAKEAWAYS

. . . . amen. ♥

date

author: _____ audience _____

Notes

written on my ♡:

life

APPLICATION

reminds ME OF:

" quotes "

Prayer + Praise

key TAKEAWAYS

. . . . amen. ♥

SCRIPTURE: _____ date _____

author: _____ audience _____

Notes

written on my ♡: _____

+ life +
APPLICATION

reminds
ME OF:

66 quotes 99

_____
_____
_____
_____
_____
_____
_____
_____
_____
_____

Prayer + Praise

key +
TAKEAWAYS

. . . . amen. ♥

SCRIPTURE: _____ date [_____]

author: _____ audience _____

Notes

written on my ♥:

life

APPLICATION

reminds

ME OF:

" quotes "

Prayer + Praise

key

TAKEAWAYS

. . . . amen. ♥

SCRIPTURE: _____ date [_____]

author: _____ audience _____

Notes

[written on my ♡:]

life

APPLICATION

reminds ME OF:

" quotes "

Prayer + Praise

key TAKEAWAYS

········ amen. ♥

SCRIPTURE: _____ date [_____]

author: _____ audience _____

Notes

written on my ♡:

+ life +
APPLICATION

reminds ME OF:

_____
_____
_____
_____
_____
_____
_____
_____
_____
_____

" quotes "

Prayer + Praise

key +
TAKEAWAYS

. . . . amen. ♥

SCRIPTURE: _____ date _____

author: _____ audience _____

Notes

+

+   +

[written on my ♥:]

life
APPLICATION

reminds ME OF:

"quotes"

_____
_____
_____
_____
_____
_____
_____
_____

Prayer + Praise

key TAKEAWAYS

· · · · · · · · amen. ♥

SCRIPTURE: _____ date [____]

author: _____ audience _____

Notes

written on my ♡:

life
APPLICATION

reminds ME OF:

66 quotes 99

Prayer + Praise

key
TAKEAWAYS

. . . . amen. ♥

SCRIPTURE: _____ date [   ]

author: _____ audience _____

Notes

written on my ♡:

+life+
APPLICATION

reminds
ME OF:

"quotes"

Prayer + Praise

key
TAKEAWAYS

.... amen. ♥

SCRIPTURE: _____ date _____

author: _____ audience _____

Notes

written on my ♡:

+ life +
APPLICATION

reminds ME OF:

66 quotes 99

Prayer + Praise

key + TAKEAWAYS

.... amen. ♥

SCRIPTURE: _____ date [____]

author: _____ audience _____

Notes

[written on my ♡:]

life

APPLICATION

reminds
ME OF:

"quotes"

_____
_____
_____
_____
_____
_____
_____
_____
_____
_____

Prayer + Praise

key
TAKEAWAYS

. . . . amen. ♥

SCRIPTURE: _____ **date** [_____]

author: _____ audience _____

Notes

written on my ♥: _____

life

+ APPLICATION

reminds ME OF:

" quotes "

Prayer + Praise

key TAKEAWAYS

. . . . amen. ♥

SCRIPTURE: _____ date [_____]

author: _____ audience _____

Notes

✝

✝   ✝

written on my ♥:

life
APPLICATION

reminds **ME OF:**

66 quotes 99

Prayer + Praise

key **TAKEAWAYS**

.... amen. ♥

SCRIPTURE: _____ date [____]

author: _____ audience _____

Notes

[written on my ♡:]

life
+ APPLICATION

reminds
ME OF:

66 quotes 99

_____
_____
_____
_____
_____
_____
_____
_____

Prayer + Praise

Key
TAKEAWAYS

. . . . *amen.* ♥

SCRIPTURE: _____ date [ ]

author: _____ audience _____

Notes

written on my ♥: [✏️]

life +
APPLICATION

reminds
ME OF:

66 quotes 99

Prayer + Praise

key +
TAKEAWAYS

.... amen. ♥

SCRIPTURE: _____ **date** [____]

author: _____ audience _____

Notes

✝

[written on my ♡:]

+ life
+ APPLICATION

reminds
ME OF:

66 quotes 99

_____
_____
_____
_____
_____
_____
_____
_____
_____

Prayer + Praise

key
TAKEAWAYS

. . . . amen. ♥

author: _____ audience _____

Notes

[written on my ♡:]

life +

APPLICATION

reminds +

ME OF:

66 quotes 99

_____
_____
_____
_____
_____
_____
_____
_____
_____

Prayer + Praise

key +

TAKEAWAYS

. . . . amen. ♥

SCRIPTURE: _____ **date** [   ]

author: _____ audience _____

Notes

written on my ♡:

+ life +

APPLICATION

reminds ME OF:

"" **quotes** ""

Prayer + Praise

key TAKEAWAYS +

. . . . amen. ♥

SCRIPTURE: _____ **date** [____]

author: _____ audience _____

Notes

✝

✝   ✝

⌐ written on my ♡: ⌐

life

APPLICATION

reminds
ME OF:

66 quotes 99

Prayer + Praise

key
TAKEAWAYS

.... amen. ♥

SCRIPTURE: _____ **date** [_____]

author: _____ audience _____

Notes

```
[ written on my ♡: ]
```

life

+ *life*

APPLICATION

reminds

ME OF:

" quotes "

Prayer + Praise

key

TAKEAWAYS

. . . . amen. ♥

author: _____ audience _____

Notes

written on my ♥:

life

APPLICATION

reminds
ME OF:

" quotes "

key
TAKEAWAYS

Prayer + Praise

. . . . amen. ♥

SCRIPTURE: _____ date [_____]

author: _____ audience _____

Notes

✝

[written on my ♥:]

+ *life*

+ APPLICATION

reminds ME OF:

_____
_____
_____
_____
_____
_____
_____
_____

" *quotes* "

Prayer + Praise

key TAKEAWAYS +

. . . . amen. ♥

SCRIPTURE: _____ date [____]

author: _____ audience _____

Notes

[written on my ♥:]

+ life
APPLICATION

reminds ME OF:

" quotes "

_____
_____
_____
_____
_____
_____
_____
_____

Prayer + Praise

key +
TAKEAWAYS

· · · · · · · amen. ♥

SCRIPTURE: _____ date [___]

author: _____ audience _____

Notes

written on my ♡:

life
+ **APPLICATION**

+ reminds
ME OF:

" quotes "

Prayer + Praise

key
TAKEAWAYS +

. . . . amen. ♥

SCRIPTURE: _____ date [____]

author: _____ audience _____

Notes

✝

✝   ✝

written on my ♡:
✏

life

APPLICATION

reminds
ME OF:

" quotes "

Prayer + Praise

key
TAKEAWAYS

. . . . amen. ♥

author: _____ audience _____

Notes

[written on my ♥:]

life
APPLICATION

reminds
ME OF:

" quotes "

Prayer + Praise

key
TAKEAWAYS

. . . . amen. ♥

SCRIPTURE: _____ date [ ]

author: _____ audience _____

Notes

written on my ♥:

life

+ APPLICATION

reminds **ME OF:**

" quotes "

Prayer + Praise

key **TAKEAWAYS**

. . . . amen. ♥

author: _____ audience _____

Notes

[written on my ♥:]

+ life
+ APPLICATION

reminds ME OF:

66 quotes 99

Prayer + Praise

key + TAKEAWAYS

. . . . amen. ♥

author: _____ audience _____

Notes

written on my ♡:

_____

+ *life*
+
APPLICATION

reminds
ME OF:

" *quotes* "

_____
_____
_____
_____
_____
_____
_____
_____
_____

Prayer + Praise

Key +
TAKEAWAYS

· · · · · · · · *amen.* ♥

SCRIPTURE: _____ date [____]

author: _____ audience _____

Notes

written on my ♡: [_____]

life

+ APPLICATION

reminds ME OF:

" quotes "

Prayer + Praise

key + TAKEAWAYS

.... amen. ♥

SCRIPTURE: _____ **date** [ ]

author: _____ audience _____

Notes

✝

✝   ✝

written on my ♥:
✏

life

APPLICATION

reminds ME OF:

66 quotes 99

key TAKEAWAYS

Prayer + Praise

. . . . amen. ♥

SCRIPTURE: _____ **date** [_____]

author: _____ audience _____

Notes

written on my ♡: [pencil]

life +

APPLICATION

reminds
ME OF:

" quotes "

_____
_____
_____
_____
_____
_____
_____
_____
_____

Prayer + Praise

Key +
TAKEAWAYS

. . . . amen. ♥

SCRIPTURE: _____ date [ ]

author: _____ audience _____

Notes

written on my ♡:

life + APPLICATION

reminds ME OF:

66 quotes 99

Prayer + Praise

key + TAKEAWAYS

. . . . amen. ♥

life

APPLICATION

" quote

key

TAKEAWAYS

Prayer + Praise

URE: _____

_____ audience _____

Notes